HORRIBLE
HISTORIES

HORRIBLE HISTORIES®

TERRY DEARY — ILLUSTRATED BY **MARTIN BROWN**

CARDIFF

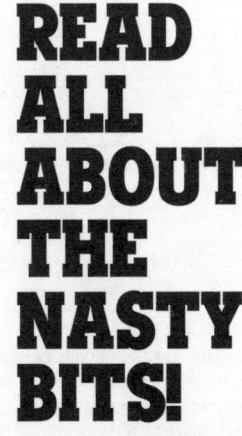

READ ALL ABOUT THE NASTY BITS!

SCHOLASTIC

While this book is based on real characters and actual historical events, some situations and people are fictional. The 'advertisements' * are entirely fictional and do not relate to any actual service or product and are not intended imply they or anything similar may exist. No 'advertisement' constitutes an endorsement, guarantee, warranty or recommendation by the publisher and the publisher does not make representations or warranties about any product or service contained or implied to be contained therein.

*Except any advertisements for the publisher's books, that is.

Published in the UK by Scholastic, 2024
Euston House, 24 Eversholt Street, London, NW1 1DB
Scholastic Ireland, 89E Lagan Road, Dublin Industrial Estate, Glasnevin, Dublin, D11 HP5F

SCHOLASTIC and associated logos are trademarks and/or
registered trademarks of Scholastic Inc.

Text © Terry Deary, 2024
Illustrations © Martin Brown, 2024

The right of Terry Deary and Martin Brown to be identified as the author and illustrator of this work has been asserted by them under the Copyright, Designs and Patents Act 1988.

ISBN 978 07023 3120 6

A CIP catalogue record for this book is available from the British Library.

All rights reserved.
This book is sold subject to the condition that it shall not, by way of trade or otherwise, be lent, hired out or otherwise circulated in any form of binding or cover other than that in which it is published. No part of this publication may be reproduced, stored in a retrieval system, or transmitted in any form or by any other means (electronic, mechanical, photocopying, recording or otherwise) without prior written permission of Scholastic Limited.

Printed and bound in Great Britain by Clays Ltd, Elcograf S.p.A.
Paper made from wood grown in sustainable forests and other controlled sources.

1 3 5 7 9 10 8 6 4 2

www.scholastic.co.uk

WHAT'S INSIDE?

EXCLUSIVE: Read about the Cardiff Castle kidnap see pages 33–35

FREE: Three ghoulish ghost stories to read just before bed see pages 87–96

INTRODUCTION p7

THE ROTTEN ROMANS p10

THE VICIOUS VIKINGS p22

THE STORMIN' NORMANS p29

THE MEASLY MIDDLE AGES p40

THE TERRIBLE TUDORS p48

THE SLIMY STUARTS p62

THE GORGEOUS GEORGIANS p75

THE VILE VICTORIANS p85

TERRIBLE 20TH CENTURY p103

EPILOGUE p119

INTERESTING INDEX p122

INTRODUCTION

Cardiff is the capital city of Wales. Wales is the land of the Red Dragon, leeks, Saint David and daffodils. A charming place…

Don't worry, it hasn't always been a pleasant place to live and die. Its history has been horrible at times.

People have been executed on the streets of Cardiff. Some have even been burned to death. The flag of Wales is the Red Dragon. Maybe it would like that?

The friars wrote down Cardiff's history in their chronicles. The fliers didn't because dragons can't write.

Between the two we can be sure that Nasty Nia will find enough horrible history to give her nightmares.

THE ROTTEN ROMANS

P eople lived in an old settlement to the west of Cardiff. Historians call it Caerau Hillfort. It was probably there at least 3,000 years ago.

DID YOU KNOW...?

The warriors in ancient Britain believed in the power of the head. They believed severed heads could help them see into the future.

They stuck rotting heads on poles at the gates of their hillforts like Caerau in Cardiff. No skulls have been found at Caerau yet. The Brits threw heads into lakes and rivers as a gift to the gods. They even nailed enemy heads to their walls as a sort of decoration.

And that's the sort of people the Romans faced when they invaded Wales…

RUTHLESS RAIDERS

The Romans were the first horrible historians to write about Wales, so we know a little about the people of South Wales from them. Monks read the Roman scripts and copied them.

Caratacus didn't want to give up the fight against the Romans. He needed to find a new army, a tribe that enjoyed fighting.

Not many Britons were keen to fight. A lot of

tribes decided it was better to make peace with the Romans.

Caratacus arrived in the area we now call Cardiff, and he found the people of Caerau Hillfort … the Silures.

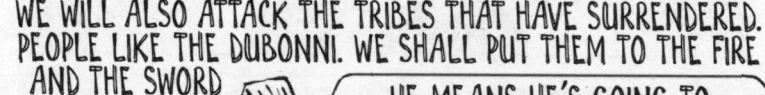

The Romans arrived in Wales looking to capture Caractacus. The Roman general Publius Ostorius

Scapula (died AD 52) wanted to battle because that's what the Romans were good at. The Silures wanted to just raid Roman camps and attack Roman supply wagons on the wild Welsh roads. This is called 'guerrilla' warfare.

By AD 50 the Silures army was weaker because of the constant war. Caratacus and his fighters moved north to get help from the Ordovices tribe. That left the ordinary Silures people in Cardiff with nobody to fight for them. General Publius Ostorius Scapula had an idea…

The savage Scapula chased Caratacus into the mountains of Wales. The rebel Brit decided this was a good place to have a full battle against the legions.

Caratacus fought a great final battle. Of course, he lost. Roman historian, Tacitus said…

It was a glorious victory. The wife and daughter of Caratacus were captured, and his brothers surrendered.

Caratacus did the same thing as he had when his own tribe were defeated: he ran away to find another tribe that would join his fight against Rome. The Brigantes.

The Brigantes – living up in the area we now call Yorkshire – had Queen Cartimandua ruling them.

But remember, a lot of British tribes were FRIENDS with the Roman invaders. Sadly, Cartimandua was one of them and Caratacus went to her for help. Another BIG mistake, Caratacus.

Cartimandua 'helped' Caratacus into shackles and chains and handed him over to the Romans.

Publius Ostorius Scapula – the enemy of the

Silures – died soon after he captured Caratacus. A Roman historian said he was...

WORN OUT WITH CARE.

He is probably buried somewhere near Cardiff.

The Silures carried on fighting, fighting, fighting even though Caratacus was gone. It took another 25 years and two more Roman generals before the Silures and Cardiff were finally crushed.

The Romans built a fort – in Welsh it's called a 'caer'. It was on the river Taff. This was the inspiration for the Silures to name the area...

Caer-Taff became Cardiff.

As for Caratacus, he was taken to Rome to be executed by being strangled to death. But Caratacus said to Emperor Claudius…

The great hero of Wales never went back to Wales. He lived happily ever after in Rome.

The Romans were rotten, but the tribes of Britain were bloodthirsty too. Those heads that they cut off would start to go mouldy and smell. They found a way to stop the brains in the dead heads rotting away.

DID YOU KNOW...?

You can visit the ruins of Caerau Hillfort. Everybody knows that.

But down in the basement of Cardiff Castle you can see a large painting. It tells the story of the invasion of Rome and the battle between the Silures and the Romans.

The Cardiff Castle you can see today was built by the Third Marquess of Bute, John Patrick Crichton-Stuart (1847–1900). His father had made his fortune building Cardiff Docks. The docks brought wealth to the town as well as to the Scottish island, Bute.

Lord Bute had a huge amount of money and wanted to build castles. In 1865 he began to restore Cardiff Castle on top of the old Roman 'caer'. He wanted it to look like a castle from the Middle Ages ... except it didn't. It has a clock tower.

Lord Bute also added running water and central heating. His wife, Gwendolen, said she would not move in without the comfort of those things. It was finished by 1877.

The Marquess had a great feast to celebrate the castle being finished. During the party in 1900 he went to a little room behind the library ... and dropped down dead. He was 53 years old.

In 1947 the family gave the castle to the people of Cardiff so you can visit it today. But beware ... Lord Bute's ghost can be seen walking through the fireplace of the library.

DID YOU KNOW...?

In Roman times there were forts built along the river Taff in Cardiff. The people were worried about attacks. From where?
   a) France
   b) Russia
   c) Ireland

Answer: **c)** Ireland. Some Irish did land and settle there. They stayed long after the Romans had roamed back to Rome.

And by 1851, there were 20,000 people in Wales who had been born in Ireland. They had escaped starvation in Ireland, so they were willing to work for a tiny amount of money. That meant they got jobs very easily, and the Welsh were thrown out of work. The Welsh had riots against the Irish in places like Cardiff.

THE VICIOUS VIKINGS

The Romans went back home around AD 410 and left Cardiff (and Britain) in the Dark Ages. The Angles and Saxons from Germany took over the East of Britain and named it 'Angle-land'. That is 'England' to you and me.

The monks had a monastery at Greyfriars. It was just down the road from Cardiff Castle.

It was peaceful until the Vicious Vikings arrived and started to raid Wales. The top monk was Saint David. The cathedral in Cardiff is named after him.

Lovely? Not everyone thought that…

DID YOU KNOW...?

It is said that Saint David was so strict that a couple of his monks planned to murder him. They poisoned his bread. The kind man fed it to a hungry dog and a crow, and they died. Only that miracle saved David.

One legend tells how Saint David made the leek the vegetable of Wales.

Killing Saxons doesn't sound very Christian.

MORE RUTHLESS RAIDERS

But the monks never had the peaceful life that you might imagine. They had to face a new terror from AD 850 to 870…

Imagine the terror of Cardiff monks in the Dark Ages. Looking out over Cardiff Bay and seeing that dreadful sight … a Viking longboat coming to plunder your monastery, make slaves of the monks … or even murder them in cold blood.

The Vikings settled on the banks of the rivers Rhymney and Taff and used the port at Cardiff to sail in and out.

The Vikings were mostly traders, selling Welsh wheat to Ireland, as well as Welsh horses. But the best trade was in Welsh slaves.

The Norse raiders told the Welsh their long poems – or sagas. If the frightened Cardiff monks had a saga about the Vikings, it may have gone a little like this (try singing it to the tune of 'Land of Hope and Glory'):

> Vikings on the horizon, coming here in their ships,
> If we do-n't start running, then we've had our chips.
> Vikings down in the bay now, big men, ugly and hairy,
> Time to start to pray now, Lord they're horribly scary.
>
> Landings hopelessly gory, we will never be free,
> How shall we escape thee, when you come from the sea?
> You will certainly kill us when you get to our village,
> With a great fear you fill us, when you come here to pillage.

Of course, if the Vikings spared the monks their song might change...

> Landings not all that gory we will ever be free,
> How shall we repay thee? Next time come and have tea.
> You did not mean to kill us, once your pillage you get,
> Lord who made thee Viking, make thee mightier yet.

THE VIKINGS VANQUISHED

The Viking forces met the Welsh and Saxon armies at the Battle of Buttington in AD 893. The Vikings were massacred.

No one is sure where that battle happened, but some historians say it may have been Chepstow, just a few miles from Cardiff. The Cardiff Vikings would have joined that battle ... and never gone home to their town on the Taff.

But by the 1070s the Welsh had a greater enemy

than the Vikings. The Normans arrived in England. Just like the Romans, the Normans headed west to squelch the Welsh. The Welsh needed warriors to fight off the Normans. Who would fight for them? Vikings.

THE STORMIN' NORMANS

William the Conqueror conquered Normandy, conquered England, conquered Wales and then he stopped.

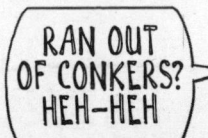

William gave land to his lords, and they paid him back by fighting for him. William marched into Cardiff in 1081 for his first and only visit.

So which lord got Cardiff?

A wooden Cardiff Castle was built for Robert Fitzhamon (1050–1107) in 1091, on the site of the Roman fort.

Robert's son-in-law, Robert, first Earl of Gloucester (1090–1147), rebuilt it in stone, including the twelve-sided tower – the keep – which can still be seen today.

William the Conqueror had squabbling sons. Robert II of Normandy (1051–1134) argued with his younger brother, King Henry I (1068–1135), who had become king of England. Robert tried to invade England to take his brother's crown. He failed and was thrown into prison from 1106 until 1134. Nearly thirty years. He spent his last few years imprisoned in Cardiff Castle.

Then he died. But he had always been trouble. He had even fought against his own father, William, and nearly killed him. As William the Conqueror might have written in his diary…

> My Robert has always been lazy and weak. Greedy too. I made him Duke of Normandy. I visited him there.

Two of my other sons — William and Henry — played a wicked joke on him. William and Henry played dice with Robert. They grew bored. They left the gaming table and crept on to the balcony above. They filled a toilet pot full of pee (and other stinking matter). They then tipped it over Robert's head. Robert didn't think it was funny.

He flew into such a rage that he attacked his brothers. I had to come between them. Robert cried like a baby and told me that I should punish them. I didn't.

His revenge was foul as that toilet pot. He tried to attack my castle at Rouen.

I joined the battle against him and met him face to face. To my shame, he knocked me off my horse and raised his sword to kill me.

When I cried out, he knew his father's face was under the helmet and he spared my life.

Robert was short of money to pay his army. Then I heard he found money to keep up the battle against me. Where did the money come from?

Oh, the shame, the bitter taste of it. The money came from his mother — my wife, my beloved Matilda.

Matilda had betrayed William the Conqueror. It broke his heart. Turning William's own wife against him – THAT is the sort of person Robert was, so you may not feel too sorry for him locked away in Cardiff Castle. But if you hear the next tale you probably WILL feel sorry.

**Horrible Histories warning.
This story is REALLY horrible...**

IN 1128 ROBERT WAS SENT TO PRISON IN CARDIFF CASTLE. IT IS SAID THAT HE TRIED TO ESCAPE BUT HIS HORSE WAS BOGGED DOWN IN A SWAMP. OF COURSE, HE WAS CAUGHT AND TAKEN BACK. TO STOP HIM ESCAPING AGAIN, KING HENRY HAD HIS BROTHER ROBERT'S EYES BURNT OUT

JUST WAIT TILL I GET MY HANDS ON THAT HORSE!

Robert died in Cardiff aged in his early 80s.

DID YOU KNOW...?

There is a story that says the bridge over the river Taff is haunted by a grey lady called Sarah. She is said to wave towards the castle, looking for Robert ... the love of her life.

CUNNING KIDNAP

In 1158 Cardiff Castle was the scene for a daring kidnapping carried out by one Ifor Bach (Ivor the Short). Ifor Bach said he was the Welsh lord of Senghenydd. But of course, the Norman Lord William had taken over.

Ifor wanted his land back.

But it was Lady Gloucester who he found there. The Cardiff newspapers would have been full of excitement at what happened next. There were NO newspapers at that time, as you know, but if there HAD been, they may have looked like this…

The Cardiff Reporter

IFOR CROSS WITH LADY GLOSS

Reports are coming in of a daring raid on Cardiff Castle by its old owner Ifor Bach. After climbing the walls, he found Lady Gloucester in her bedroom. Servants report hearing her scream, 'Who's there? William. William. There's someone in the room. Let me light a candle – where's the tinder box…'

Ifor Bach replied, 'Don't scream, Lady Gloss, or I may have to cut your throat. And you are more use to me alive.' He went on, 'This is MY land, and your husband stole it from me.'

The French wife of Lord Gloucester cried, 'Stole? No. He is the rightful Lord – the king conqueror said so.'

'I don't care what your Norman king says. He can't mess with me,' It seems Ifor didn't understand everything she said. Ifor turned nasty.

He threatened to cut her son's throat if her husband didn't sign over the land to him. 'I would kill him very slowly – and probably let you watch. Then I'd kill your husband even more slowly. And finally, I'd kill you so very slowly you'll beg me for death. How does that sound, my lady?'

'A bit messy to be honest,' she replied.

He threatened to take her with him, and hold her hostage until Bach was back finally back on his land.

The latest reports say the Duke of Gloucester has agreed to give back Bach's land. So, hijack Bach wins.

CASTLE HASSLE

The Clare family lived in Cardiff Castle from 1217. Gilbert de Clare, the fifth Earl of Gloucester, was one of the barons who had made King John sign *Magna Carta*. That was a treaty where England's King John agreed to behave himself and give his barons more power.

Cardiff Castle isn't the only castle in the area. There is also Castell Coch – the 'Red Castle' – just outside Cardiff on the Merthyr Road. It looks like a fairy-tale castle with its pointy towers. It was built in the 1080s by the Normans. The ruthless lord Gilbert de Clare, the seventh Earl of Gloucester (1243–95) lived there. He was known as 'Red' Gilbert de Clare or 'the Red Earl', because of his hair colour. And also because of his fiery temper and bloodthirsty ways. Here are some facts about this nasty Norman…

• Gilbert joined his mate Simon de Montfort as a rebel against the English King Henry III.

• They fought against the king and beat him in 1264 when the king surrendered. Gilbert married the king's niece, Alice.

• In 1264 he led an attack on the Jews in Canterbury. His lordly friends owed Canterbury money-lenders money. Gilbert's men beat and even killed some of the Jewish bankers, then burned their homes. The Normans kept the Jews' money, of course.

• Gilbert grew jealous of his pal Simon de Montfort who was growing famous and powerful. So, Gilbert switched sides and fought FOR the king at the battle of Evesham, where his mate was now his enemy.

• Simon was killed with a lance to the throat before Gilbert's friends hacked him to death.

• Gilbert was always quarrelling with the lords next door. He argued with the Bishop of Hereford … over what?

a) An evil witch
b) A border ditch
c) A football pitch

Answer: **b)** Gilbert spent a lot of money and built Castell Coch just five miles north of Cardiff Castle. Two castles in five miles sounds a bit of a Greedy Gilbert. He hardly spent any time at Castell Coch because he was always off smashing people. Castell Coch was wrecked in the early 1300s by rebels. Its walls were tumbling into a ruin.

DID YOU KNOW...?

One of the Castle Coch dungeons became a bottomless pool. One day a boy went exploring and fell in. His mother's wandering, wailing ghost still haunts the place.

It doesn't look like a ruin today because it was restored by the Marquess of Bute in the 1880s, just three years after he started rebuilding Cardiff Castle. Lord Bute never liked it much. Probably too spooky.

There were paintings on the ceilings, but Lord Bute was angry at the picture of monkeys over his wife's bed. He said they were too rude.

DID YOU ALSO KNOW....?

In the 1640s one of King Charles I's army hid his treasure in a secret passage at Castle Coch. This passage ran all the way to Cardiff Castle. Maybe Charles's ghost is seeking the treasure? His ghost haunts the castle and has driven away the last person to live there. No one has ever found the treasure.

Of course, King Charles had his head chopped off by his enemies in 1649. It is very difficult to find treasure when you have no head.

DID YOU ALSO ALSO KNOW....?

Some people say the treasure belongs to Ifor Bach – the man who climbed the walls of Cardiff Castle.

The treasure is guarded by two eagles who'll kill you if you try to steal it. And they can't be killed – even with a silver bullet.

Castell Coch was used as a camp for soldiers in the Second World War. Gilbert the Red would have liked that.

THE MEASLY MIDDLE AGES

Cardiff was a lawless place in the Middle Ages. It was infested with pirates who sailed up the Bristol Channel.

The Welsh were revolting again in 1316. This time under Llywelyn Bren (died 1318) … who came to a very sticky end in Cardiff.

Trials always make good drama. Here is a playscript for you to try…

SCRIPT

JUDGE: I am the judge Hugh Despenser. Bring in the accused. You are Llywelyn Bren?

LLYWELYN BREN: That's me. Great-grandson of the famous Ifor Bach who famously took this castle single handed.

JUDGE: Famous rebels and troublemakers, the lot

of you. You are here to be given a fair trial, after which you will be found guilty and executed.

LLYWELYN BREN: How's that fair?

JUDGE: Now, how do you plead?

LLYWELYN BREN: Not guilty.

JUDGE: (Banging his table) I hereby sentence you to...

LLYWELYN BREN: Hang on, hang on. You haven't heard my side of the story yet.

JUDGE: Llywelyn Bren, you were charged with treason. You gathered an army and started attacking all the castles around Cardiff. You even burned Cardiff.

LLYWELYN BREN: Not really. I just singed bits of it to the north.

JUDGE: Singed it? Repairs to the walls cost three pounds, thirteen shillings and one farthing.

LLYWELYN BREN: I'll pay for the damage the lads did...

JUDGE: So, you admit it. I hereby sentence you to...

LLYWELYN BREN: Hang on, hang on. I had my reasons.
JUDGE: I hereby sentence you to...
LLYWELYN BREN: Wait! There has been a terrible famine in Wales for a year. The peasants are starving yet the king still forced them to pay their taxes. I was just making a protest for the sake of the good people of Cardiff.

JUDGE: Protest? In one castle you massacred all the soldiers inside.
LLYWELYN BREN: Yeah, well they were trying to kill us. My favourite horse was killed in one raid. Anyway, I gave myself up when the English army arrived. I stood in front of my troops — as I stand in front of this court now — and I made my famous speech to my men. Men, I said, this was my war so I will give myself up for my people. It is better that one man should die than a whole nation should suffer.

JUDGE: Sounds like treason to me. I hereby sentence you to be hanged, drawn and quartered.

LLYWELYN BREN: You what? King Edward said I should just be hanged.

JUDGE: That was before you burned Cardiff. First you are drawn round Cardiff on a wooden sledge. Then you are hanged a little bit till you are not quite dead. Then you are stretched out and your belly is cut open.

LLYWELYN BREN: I bet that makes my eyes water.

JUDGE: Your guts are pulled out. They are burned on the fire in front of your eyes.

JUDGE: Then we cut off your head and chop your body into quarters.

LLYWELYN BREN: Nasty. Couldn't you do the head cutting first and the painful bits after?

JUDGE: Come on, Llywelyn Bren. Chop-chop.

LLYWELYN BREN: Where are we going?

JUDGE: It's time to . . . head off.

LLYWELYN BREN: That's horrible history.

Llywelyn Bren had been friends with Gilbert Clare, the Norman lord of the Cardiff area – Glamorgan. But in 1314 Gilbert died, and the new lord, Payne de Turberville, took over in 1315. Payne did NOT like Llywelyn Bren.

Llywelyn Bren led a rebellion of the Welsh people in the hills outside Cardiff. They were NEVER going to win against the Norman lords. Llywelyn Bren was locked in the Tower of London for a year but taken back to Cardiff to be executed ... 'Payne-fully'.

Payne de Turberville wanted the Welsh people to see what would happen to anyone who tried to rebel.

The Welsh have a long history of people who rebelled against their harsh lives of hard work and hunger.

DID YOU KNOW....?

In 1795 a group of Welsh miners led a revolt against their brutal lives. The revolt was quickly crushed by the government. It led to the deaths of several miners. Miners in Hook took the law into their own hands and rioted in the west. They were never going to win against the British army.

Llywelyn Bren and his head were buried in Greyfriars Monastery graveyard.

Just eighty years after Llywelyn Bren, the rebel Owain Glyndŵr (1354 to about 1415) arrived, and he burned Cardiff really badly.

That is true. Of course, Hywel was from a different branch of the family … tree … branch … get it? Oh, never mind.

Just on the west edge of Cardiff there was a castle at Peterston-super-Ely. Owain Glyndŵr surrounded it. Owain Glyndŵr called to the castle keeper, 'Surrender.'

The castle keeper thought, *'If I surrender, I'll save lots of lives from a battle.'* He surrendered. Owain Glyndŵr cut off his head.

In the end Owain Glyndŵr was beaten by the English and disappeared. At least he wasn't butchered like Llywelyn Bren.

THE TERRIBLE TUDORS

You would think things would get better for the people of Cardiff and Wales when Henry Tudor invaded. After all, he was from a Welsh family.

In 1485 Henry Tudor landed in Wales and marched across to England where he met King Richard III in battle. Henry Tudor won and became King Henry VII.

As Henry was king he could make a great Welsh leader the Lord of Cardiff. Who did Henry VII choose to be Lord of Cardiff in 1488?

a) The Welsh Prince Hugh, who had saved Cardiff from Richard III's armies
b) The poor but kindly woman called Eleanor, who looked after Cardiff Castle and the poor
c) His uncle, Jasper Tudor

Answer: c) If you were a Tudor king you could give the town and its people to anyone you liked.

FAMILY FORTUNES

Uncle Jasper was the most important person who helped Henry VII snatch the throne from Richard III. One of his rewards was to be given Cardiff. If there had been no Jasper Tudor, there would probably have been no Terrible Tudors ruling England.

Jasper had helped to bring up Henry VII after young Henry lost his father.

Jasper lost his own father too. After Jasper and his dad, Owen, lost a battle, his dad was captured.

Owen THOUGHT he would be locked in prison. He was surprised when he was taken out and had his head put on a block.

Some people like surprises. Owen's head was cut off and stuck on top of the stone market cross in Hereford. A report at the time said…

A mad woman combed his hair and washed away the blood on his face.

Jasper must have been glad his dad's head was looked after.

Jasper had seen lots of death and violence all his life. After his nephew Henry VII took the throne, Jasper married Catherine. She was a widow. Guess what happened to her first husband?

Jasper was known for being cunning. He was once trapped in a castle, surrounded by an enemy army. He dressed as a peasant and walked out – the enemy didn't know who he was.

Jasper died in 1495. His guts were buried in the nearby church. The rest of his body was buried 20 miles away in Keynsham abbey. Weird.

There isn't much sign that a great Tudor was once Lord of Cardiff. But he paid to have a tower built at Llandaff Cathedral. It is named the Jasper Tower.

NOT-SO-GREAT EIGHT

Henry VII's Tudor family reigned for over 100 years. But they did no good for Wales. Henry's son, the monstrous Henry VIII, passed a law called the Act of Union in 1536. Wales was to be ruled by England.

King Henry VIII closed down all the abbeys, robbed them and flattened them but his great uncle – Jasper Tudor – was buried at an abbey. Did Henry leave that abbey alone?

Never mind, you can still visit the grave of Jasper's guts in Thornbury.

Henry VIII closed down Greyfriars monastery in Cardiff in the 1530s, and about 40 years later it was bought by the Herbert family, who pulled it down. They used the stones to build a house in the centre of Cardiff.

In 1967 that house was pulled down to build that ugly great tower block, Capital Tower.

After Henry VIII's Act of Union everyone had to speak English if they wanted to get on.

MEAN STREETS

Wales was a lawless place at the end of the Tudor age. Laws were broken and people got away with it.

In Cardiff there were street brawls in 1577 with women as well as men involved. One report said this…

HIGH STAKES

Henry VIII wanted rid of the power of the Catholic Church. He wanted England and Wales to be Protestant.

So did Thomas Capper. But Capper was the wrong sort of Protestant for Henry.

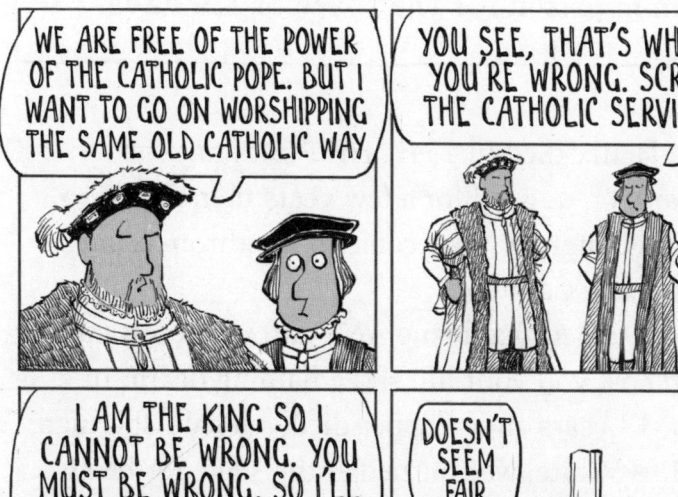

In 1542 Thomas Capper was burned at the stake in Cardiff for 'heresy'. He was first person to die for his religion since Roman times. And that was daft because he was a Protestant, just like King Henry VIII.

An old document in Cardiff said…

> This is a record of a payment of 4 shillings and 4 pence as the costs of burning Thomas Capper and of keeping him in prison for the space of 130 days.

Then Henry died in 1547. His Protestant son, Edward VI, reigned for a few years then died, too. Henry's daughter Mary came to the throne. And Mary was a Catholic.

She decided that being ANY sort of Protestant could cost you your life and a flaming death. In 1555, 13 years after Capper died, a local fisherman, Rawlins White, was burned at the stake for being a Protestant.

White had been a fisherman in the town for over 20 years. He lived between the river Taff and Westgate Street, near where the Millennium Stadium now stands.

Rawlins White had probably learned to be a Protestant from same preachers who had taught Thomas Capper.

A report said…

> *Rawlins White was a good man … with no schooling and very simple. Still, he was a great searcher-out of truth.*

Rawlins sent his son to school so he could read the Bible to him. Everyone seemed to like him. But Queen Mary didn't like his religion.

Rawlins was kept in Cardiff Castle before being taken out and burned at St Mary's Street.

In prison he asked for his wife to bring him his best shirt. It was the one in which he had been married, and the shirt in which he would have been buried upon his death.

On his way to the stake, Rawlins White saw his wife and children waiting for him by the side of the road, weeping. The sight of his family was more painful than anything.

The wood and hay were placed around the stake. White reached out to help them arrange the materials for the fire to try to make sure the flames would be large and fast.

Rawlins White was around 60 years old.

Mary Tudor was on the throne of England for five years. In that time 280 Protestants lost their lives in England and Wales, including 55 women, and some children.

DID YOU KNOW....?

In 1584, Rice Jones of Gelligaer was taken to court in Cardiff for playing tennis when he should have been at a church service. He went from court to court.

By the time the last Tudor, Elizabeth I died, Cardiff was described by a Welsh historian as…

> THE FAIREST TOWN IN WALES BUT NOT THE WEALTHIEST.
>
> GEORGE OWEN (1602)

PIRATE JOHN CALLIS

Pirates did not want to live all their lives out at sea. They wanted to go ashore and spend their loot. But if they landed they could be arrested and hanged. So where could they land safely?

HAS TO BE CARDIFF BECAUSE THAT'S WHAT THIS BOOK IS ABOUT. BUT WHY RISK IT?

BECAUSE THE JUDGES AND THE GREAT FAMILIES OF THE TOWN WERE ALL PART OF THE PIRATES' TRADE. THE RICH CARDIFF FOLK GOT A SHARE OF THE PIRATE PRIZES

In the middle of the 1500s, the pirate John Callis was married to the daughter of Nicholas Herbert, who came from an important family. But the people he robbed were mostly the French who were furious. The French forced the law officers in Cardiff to hunt down Callis.

Callis tried to hide in pubs and houses. In the end he was caught and thrown into jail. He came up with a plan…

It is said that Queen Elizabeth I gave Callis a pardon so long as he kept quiet about her officers who were mixed up in the pirate trade.

Callis owed a lot of money to some violent men. He ran away to North Africa to escape them. It is said he died in a sea battle there. Other history writers say he was hanged in Newport, a city to the east of Cardiff.

One thing is certain. He is dead.

ODD FACT

The Rummer Tavern in Duke Street, Cardiff, was built in the 1700s. It was built on a burgage plot – a narrow strip of the king's land rented to a business in the town.

Over the years, several staff and customers are said to have seen ghostly figures there, usually in the toilets and the cellar.

THE SLIMY STUARTS

Elizabeth I was the last of the Terrible Tudors and when she died in 1603 the Slimy Stuart family took over.

They got off to a bad start in Cardiff. In 1607

Cardiff was hit by 'The Great Flood'. It washed away old St. Mary's Church. Today St. Mary Street is named after the ancient church even though it's not there.

The church foundations were washed away and so were the graves in the churchyard. Corpses and skeletons floated through the streets of Cardiff till they were washed away into the river Taff.

Some people say the flood was really a tsunami wave, or tidal bore, that swept up the Bristol Channel.

DEAD FAMOUS

There is a junction on the corner of Crwys Road and Richmond Road in Roath, Cardiff, known as Death Junction. This is not because it could be car-crushed in rush hour.

The reason for its nasty name is because in 1679 two Catholic priests, Philip Evans and John Lloyd, were hanged, drawn and quartered on that spot for treason for preaching.

PHILIP EVANS (1645-79)

Philip was a Catholic who wanted to bring back the old religion to Cardiff. He went there to preach. Nobody took much notice for four years. But then there was a big scare in Britain that the Catholics were going to lead a revolution.

A judge called John Arnold set out to hunt down Catholic priests. He offered a reward...

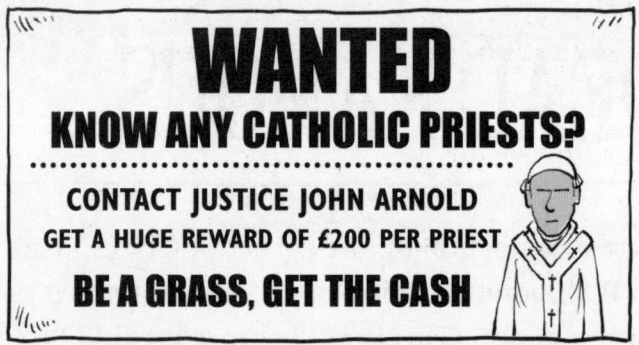

Today that £200 would be worth over £30,000.

Philip Evans was captured and locked in Cardiff Prison along with...

JOHN LLOYD (1630-79)

John was a little older than Philip Evans. His older brother William was locked up too, but died in prison from his bad treatment.

John and Philip were locked up together and became friends for the last seven months of their lives.

The trial was a joke.

NOV 1678 The Cardiff Courier

INSIDE I'VE GOT GHOSTS IN MY LOO! HAUNTED LAV TRUE STORY

TERRIBLE TRAITORS TRIED

The Catholic priests Lloyd and Evans were taken before the judge today. The first witness was a poor old woman. She was asked if she had seen them preaching a Catholic service. 'Yes,' she replied.

WITNESS

She asked the judge, 'Now are you going to give me the £50 reward for saying that?'

The judge said HE would not pay her 50 pennies. But there was a £50 reward offered by Mr John Arnold.

He sentenced the two men to be executed and told them to come back to court in three months' time.

The two traitors were sent home to wait. The *Cardiff Courier* is shocked. Lock them up, we say. They could run away.

The men didn't run away. Anyone else would have. At last, they were taken to Cardiff Prison. John had a friendly jailer who let him into the jailyard to play tennis. He was playing tennis one day when he was told he was going to be executed the next day.

He didn't make a racket.

The men were allowed to finish the game. Then they were taken back to their cell and chained to the wall. John Lloyd was able to write to his sister, Catherine Barbara, who was a nun in Paris. She kept the letter for the rest of her life.

> Dear Sister,
> I know that you will not to be at all shocked when you know that your loving brother writes this last letter unto you. In a few hours' time I shall suffer as a priest for God's sake. I hope God will welcome me into heaven. What greater happiness can a Christian man have?

The next day the friends died. Philip went first. John was forced to watch the terrible suffering. Philip spoke to the crowds in Welsh and English. He joked…

He turned to John and said…

John made no speech. He simply said…

Philip was hanged till he was half dead, had his guts cut out and finally was beheaded. John Lloyd had to watch before he suffered the same way.

In 1878 their bones were found hidden in the attic of a Catholic house in Holywell. in 1929, a stained-glass window with an image of the two priests was put up in Saint Peter's church, Cardiff. It is there to remind visitors of the two brave men.

In 1970 the Pope made both men saints.

At Death Junction there are plaques on the wall of a bank to remember the place where the two men died.

For a hundred years after the deaths of Saint John and Saint Philip there were more hangings at that spot.

ROTTEN WRECKERS

People in the savage 1600s weren't just into treason – they were into more common crimes too. Wales was still a lawless place in the age of the Stuarts.

The trouble was that the lawmakers were the biggest crooks of all.

Around the Welsh coast there were bands of 'wreckers'. In the 1600s Walter Vaughan lived here. The Vaughan family owned castles along the coast and were wealthy lords of Glamorgan. Walter Vaughan could be a cruel man in the courts…

The thief, Matthew, had an iron hand fitted and became known as Matt of the Iron Hand.

But Walter Vaughan wasted his family fortune on wild living and found himself hard up. That's when he came up with a villainous plan. He called Matt of the Iron Hand to the Castle one day…

Of course, if the shipwrecked sailors lived they could report Matthew and his gang who would hang. Vaughan said there must be no survivors. Anyone who swam ashore from the wreck would be thrown back into the sea … after the wreckers had robbed the corpse.

But the evil plot gave Vaughan a nasty shock. Matt turned up with a fine wrecking prize. But

Matt said the finest loot came from a man who was washed ashore ... alive.

Matt finished him off, just as Vaughan had ordered. The hook-handed man said he noticed the victim had a valuable ring on his hand. He couldn't get the ring off, so he cut off the hand. Vaughan asked to see it. Matt pulled it out of a bag.

Walter Vaughan never recovered, they say. He took to drinking and wandering the beach where his son was murdered.

Some say you can still see the young man's cloak floating in the water.

PUTRID PIRATES

The wreckers on the Welsh coasts didn't just wreck trading ships of course. There is a terrible tale about a pirate called Colyn Dolphyn.

A funny name. Not a very funny man. Dolphyn

was a ruthless kidnapper. But one of Colyn's victims escaped. The victim lured the pirate on to rocks near St. Donats and captured Dolphyn who was sentenced to die.

Some say Dolphyn was burned alive at Llantwit Major and others say he was buried up to his neck on the beach. When the tide came, in it was one drowned Dolphyn.

But the people of Cardiff didn't give him much. Charles started to lose the war, so Cardiff switched sides to fight with the Roundheads. The people of Cardiff let the Roundheads take control in 1646.

And THEN they rebelled for the king two years later. They couldn't make their minds up.

Switching back to the king's side didn't work for them. The king's Cardiff army was smashed in a battle in the village of St. Fagan, just outside of Cardiff. It would be last great battle ever to take place in Wales.

DID YOU KNOW...?

Caerphilly Castle is just six miles north of Cardiff. Princess Alice, niece of King Henry III, lived there.

While her husband, Lord de Clare was away, Alice fell in love with a Welshman, Tew Teg. But they were betrayed by a priest. Alice's angry husband sent her away. She must have been upset and missing her love Tew Teg.

Maybe they wrote to each other.

My dearest Alice,

No more palace for my Alice? That priest Tegwyn is a rat. Why did he tell your husband about us? For money, that's why. I hate him. Hate him, hate him. But not any longer. You will be pleased to hear I hunted him down and murdered him. The beast of a priest is gone. The man of the church has been knocked off his perch.

I can't wait to see you again. Don't worry, I'll have washed the priest's blood off my hands.

Your loving boyfriend, Tew Teg

But the lovers never met again and Alice was sent away to France. It's said that she then died of a broken heart. Now Alice haunts the palace. You can see her as a ghostly Green Lady at Caerphilly Castle. In the Civil War the Roundheads tried to blow it up. So, it now has a famous tower that leans MORE than the famous Leaning Tower of Pisa.

The Civil War ended, and it went back to being dangerous for Catholics like John Lloyd and Philip Evans.

THE GORGEOUS GEORGIANS

COAL GOLD

In 1714 the last of the Stuarts, Queen Anne, died. George I from Hanover in Germany took the throne and was the first of the gorgeous Georgians. Their family ruled until 1837 when Victoria took over.

Huge amounts of coal were discovered in the Welsh Valleys to the north of Cardiff. And the world wanted coal as well as the iron that was found there.

The mine owners would be rich of course. But so would the people who could carry the coal. If the coal went through the docks in Cardiff then Cardiff would be rich.

But the Cardiff roads were terrible. In 1782, an officer at Cardiff Docks said that…

The Bute family owned a lot of that coal. Their first answer was to build a canal that linked Cardiff to the coal and iron town of Merthyr Tydfil. In 1793, John Crichton-Stuart, the Second Marquess of Bute was born.

He spent his life building the Cardiff Docks and was later called:

The creator of modern Cardiff

In the 1830s steam trains had been invented and the Bute family built many railways to link the wealth of the valleys with the docks. So, they owned...

- The coal
- The railways to carry it to Cardiff
- The docks to take it round the world

Any ONE of those would make them a fortune.

People flocked to Cardiff like Welsh sheep to work on the coal and iron trade and the docks. Cardiff grew and grew.

It was not a safe place to live. Violence and street fighting were quite common in the dock area. Gangs of men battled, and riots were seen as normal.

There were lots of reports of terrible drunkenness.

And those people wanted a bit of fun. Their idea of fun would not be funny to us.

BULL-BAITING

At the western end of Queen Street, Cardiff, there is a statue of Aneurin Bevan (1897–1960). He was a Welshman who was famous because he helped to set up the National Health Service in Britain.

His statue stands on the spot where there used to be a bull-baiting ring.

A visitor to England described the cruel 'sport' which must have been similar to Cardiff's baiting…

> First a young ox or bull was led in and fastened by a long rope to an iron ring in the middle of the yard; then about 30 dogs, two or three at a time, were let loose on him but he made short work of them, goring them and tossing them high in the air above the height of the first storey. Several had such a grip of the bull's throat or ear that their mouths had to be forced open with poles.
>
> Finally another bull appeared, on whom several firecrackers had been hung: when these were lit and several dogs let loose on him on a sudden, there was a monstrous hurly-burly. And thus was concluded this truly English sport, which vastly delights this nation but to me seemed nothing very special.

SO HORRIBLY CRUEL AND WRONG. BUT HAVING SAID THAT, I'D LIKE SOMEONE TO LET SEVERAL DOGS LOOSE ON THESE DAMN SEAGULLS

The 'sport' was banned because it was dangerous to the public, not because it was cruel to the animals.

In Cardiff in 1773, one person went to see dogs thrown in the air by the bull. But the bull got its horns into the man instead and killed him.

DEADLY FOR DIC

One man who died in 1831 as a result of the lawless Welsh towns was Dic Penderyn (born around 1807).

The Welsh ironworkers and miners wanted to protest against the dreadful conditions they had to live in. Tiny houses crammed together, disease and filth everywhere. Merthyr was cramped with 22,000 people. Twenty-five years before there had only been 7,000. No wonder the poor ironworkers wanted things to change.

In 1831 those coal and iron workers had a riot up in Merthyr. Six soldiers were wounded but

24 rioters were killed. Dic Penderyn was charged with trying to murder a soldier by stabbing him in the leg.

A Cardiff newspaper could have reported his end like this…

THE CARDIFF BUGLE

Saturday 13 August 1831

DIC DIES DECLARING 'I DIDN'T DO IT'

Today was the last day for Richard Lewis – commonly known as Dic Penderyn. He was hanged at St. Mary Street, outside Cardiff Castle in front of a large crowd.

Dic was part of the Merthyr Riots back in May. The ironworkers of Merthyr went on a march for a better wage and to try to get the vote. It was said that they marched into Merthyr, broke into houses, and robbed them.

One man in the Merthyr crowd said those reports were not true. The man, known as Huw, said, 'We weren't robbers. The law officers had taken away our furniture because we owed money. We were just taking it back.'

The ironworkers went on to raid the courtroom, steal the court records and burn them in the streets. Huw went on, 'There was no need to send in the army. They shot 24 of the workers dead.'

But several soldiers were also wounded and that's what led to the trials. Twenty-eight men and women were put on trial.

They all ended up being sentenced to transportation to Australia. But for some reason Dic was sentenced to hang. Penderyn was found guilty of stabbing a soldier – but even the soldier said he couldn't be sure Penderyn was the man who'd stabbed him.

It's said that the two men who accused Penderyn weren't even in court. They were two hairdressers. But Dic had just had an argument with them. They hated him.

Still, he died bravely. Dic Penderyn, hands tied behind his back, was led on to the scaffold by a minister. Dic called 'O Arglwydd, dyma ganwedd.' Our Welsh readers will know that means, 'I am going to suffer unjustly.'

The hangman placed a white bag over Penderyn's head and tied his feet. He pulled the lever and there was a gasp from the crowd.

As the man Huw said, 'Dic Penderyn – a Welsh martyr'.

Poor Dic was only 23 years old, and he was innocent. Dic Penderyn was the only one of the rioters to be sentenced to death. The rest were sent to Australia.

Dic would die in Cardiff so the Merthyr people would not riot if Dic was executed near his home. Lord Melbourne was in charge of the law, and he wanted at least one rebel to die to teach the workers a lesson.

Forty years after the hanging a man called Ieuan Parker confessed, on his death bed, that he was the one who stabbed the soldier all those years ago.

Dic is remembered as a hero of the ironworkers. But in fact, Dic was a coal miner.

The hanging took place in St. Mary Street – where the Central Market now stands – and Dic was executed crying that he was innocent.

DID YOU KNOW....?

Miners like Dic Penderyn were angry because their lives were miserable. A writer called George Borrow visited the area in 1854, 23 years after Dic died, and wrote...

'To the south rose stacks of chimneys surrounded by grimy hellish-looking buildings; near by were huge heaps of cinders and black rubbish. From the chimneys smoke was gushing out even though it was Sunday.

Smoke was choking the air all around this horrid filthy place, part of which was swamp and part pool: the pool black as soot, and the swamp a disgusting lead colour.

Across this place of filth stretched a tramway.

After having seen all that I wanted, I went back to my inn and paid my bill. I then left and turned, heading eastward towards England.'

By the time Borrow visited Wales, Queen Victoria was on the throne in the horrible age of the Vile Victorians.

THE VILE VICTORIANS

The reign of the Gorgeous Georgians ended when William IV died in 1837 and Queen Victoria took the throne ... and she would stay there for over 60 years.

New queen, same dirty old Cardiff. In 1842 cholera first struck. A doctor could tell you…

CHOLERA IS A WICKED LITTLE GERM THAT LIVES IN YOUR GUTS. IT KILLS MOST OF THE PEOPLE WHO CATCH IT. YOUR POO TURNS TO WATER AND POURS OUT OF YOUR BOTTOM. AT THE OTHER END YOU KEEP VOMITING. YOUR SKIN TURNS BLUE AND THEN YOU DIE … IF YOU DON'T GET TREATED

It's caused by dirty water. Germs can also spread to food if people don't wash their hands after using the toilet. The food eaten at the funeral of a cholera victim is a great way of spreading the disease.

DID YOU KNOW…?

Thousands of Irish Catholics had come across to Cardiff to escape the famine. They caught cholera and died. Out of the famine frying pan into the cholera fire.

CARDIFF GHOST STORY 1 – THE CARDIFF CASTLE CHOLERA MYSTERY

1. On 23 May 1849, Megan Thomas arrived in Cardiff to meet her father, Tegwyn, at the docks. He'd been away to Southeast Asia as a sailor on a clipper ship and was coming home to Cardiff for some leave.

2. She began to walk him home, but as they reached the walls of the castle, Tegwyn complained that he felt ill. His legs gave way, and his breathing became harsh. His daughter later reported that she thought there was a bluish tinge to his skin.

3. She ran to find a doctor who called for an ambulance. The horse-drawn vehicle arrived after almost an hour and Megan was disturbed to notice it was numbered 13 – she was a superstitious girl.

4. The two ambulance-men were easy to remember too. The younger one had a face scarred by some disease, while the old, round-shouldered partner was totally bald.

5. The men loaded the old sailor on to the ambulance but said sorry, there was no room in the ambulance for Megan. The girl was never to see her father again – dead or alive. She wanted to get home and report to her mother anyway.

6. The next day Megan and her mother walked to the hospital and asked about the sailor who had collapsed at Cardiff Castle. The hospital said that no such patient had been treated.

7. The worried women went to the police. The police said that there was no proof that Tegwyn Thomas had ever been in Cardiff. They couldn't waste time looking for a man who may never have landed. When the women made a fuss, a police inspector visited the hospital.

8. The ambulances were lined up. There were 19 of them, numbered 1 to 20 – but there was no number 13. The senior surgeon admitted superstitious patients didn't want to travel in an ambulance with an unlucky number.

9. The surgeon also said they had never had two drivers like the men who collected Tegwyn the day before.

10. Megan returned home and told her story to the Cardiff newspaper, but the story was ignored in Cardiff. Why? And what was the explanation?

Solve the mystery ... explanation 1:

• The clues lie in Tegwyn's journey ... and the colour of his skin. A blue shade is one of the signs of cholera. If Tegwyn Thomas had contracted cholera in Southeast Asia then he would die.

• Maybe the ambulance staff who'd been in contact with him would have been put in the same cholera ward at the hospital. They could well have died too. Ambulance 13 would be burned to stop the disease spreading.

- Why did the police lie? If word got out that a cholera case had landed in Cardiff the whole port would be closed for a month or more. Thousands of people would be out of work – trade in the huge coal and iron fields of the valleys would go to Cardiff's great rivals in Newport, Swansea and Bristol.

- Thousands of people who needed the docks for money would be idle and starve. If the police hushed up his disease the port could survive the disaster. The police were told to lie. And it worked.

Solve the mystery ... explanation 2:

- Some reports said that Tegwyn Thomas was a violent and drunken man who had been known to attack his wife and daughter when in a rage.

- Did Tegwyn attack Megan on the dockside and did she kill him as she tried to defend herself?

- Maybe some sailors felt sorry for her.

- Maybe Megan and the sailors made sure Tegwyn ended up at the bottom of Cardiff Bay.

- Megan would then invent the fantastic story of Ambulance 13 to hide her guilty secret.

You decide. But remember, it is true that in May 1849, a cholera epidemic broke out in Cardiff. The disease killed 383 people. But one good thing came out of it: the town passed new laws to make sure everyone had cleaner water.

DID YOU KNOW...?

There are other haunted hospital stories in Cardiff.

Cardiff Royal Infirmary

It has been called Britain's most haunted hospital. It was built back in the 1880s.

It has been said that a priest was called in to exorcise the buildings.

Most ghostly stories are from 100 or more years ago. But there are also more modern claims. Some of the last patients at the hospital said they'd seen old-fashioned-looking nurses wandering the building.

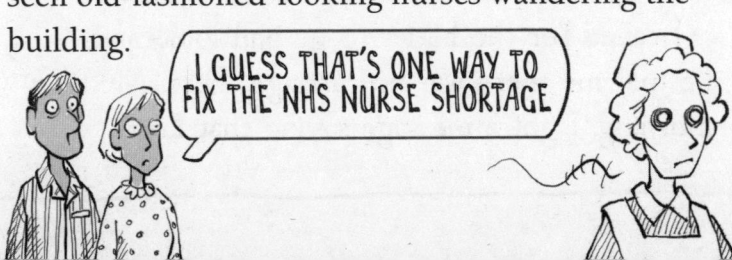

Llandough Hospital

A nurse once said she saw her own dead body in Llandough Hospital, and later that night she died. There have also been sightings of nurses in Victorian uniforms – though the hospital was built in the 1930s so it's curious as to why they'd be there.

CARDIFF GHOST STORY 2 – HORRIBLE HASTINGS

The Marquess of Bute rebuilt the old Cardiff Castle, as you know.

But in 1868 he was shocked when his cousin, the Marquess of Hastings, died at the age of 26.

Bute had gone up to Scotland and left John Boyle in charge. Boyle's ghostly tale is still believed by some...

> I was expecting a friend for dinner. I was sitting in the library, waiting, and I heard a carriage roll through the courtyard and stop at the door. I waited for my friend to ring the bell. I waited till I was sure that the bell must be broken.
>
> I called for the butler to go and look, and he told me there was no carriage there. Next morning, I got a message saying that Lord

> Hastings had died suddenly the night before ... at just the time I heard the carriage.
>
> I remembered the ancient story: if a phantom carriage is heard then it means one of the Bute family will die. I swear it is true.

Now that may seem like a simple coincidence for John Boyle. But Lord Bute died in 1900. Lady Margaret MacRae (Bute's only daughter) said that her father died in his Scottish home. At the time he died she too heard the ghostly carriage in Cardiff Castle.

DID YOU KNOW...?

Other ghosts haunt Cardiff Castle:
1. The second Marquess of Bute (who walks through several walls – apparently).
2. A faceless woman in a long skirt who is known as Sarah.
3. A 3-metre tall giant who walks around the park.

CARDIFF GHOST STORY 3 – THE BOATMAN'S TALE

A lot of ghosts are of rich people in old houses and castles. But poor people haunt the world too. See if you believe the old man's tale.

Sit by the fire and let me tell you my tale.

It happened in Cardiff, down by the river Ely. One evening an old man wandered into my bar in Leckwith, near Cardiff. He ordered a brandy and I served him. He looked frail and unwell as I poured him his drink.

I said, 'If you don't mind I'll join you. I'm freezing behind that bar. Don't know what's the matter with me. It's like someone walked over my grave.'

And he said, 'Maybe they did.'

He swallowed the brandy and shook.

'You don't believe those superstitions, do you?' I asked.

'I didn't until tonight,' he replied. And he told me his story. 'I was walking down the road from Canton. I was at the loneliest stretch when it started to get dark very quickly. Suddenly a man appeared out of nowhere and started to walk alongside me. I slowed down to let him get ahead.'

'Well, you do, don't you?'
I nodded.

'But he stayed by my side,' the old man went on. 'Then I sped up and he went faster too. I couldn't shake him off. "What do you want?" I cried.'

'And what did he say?' I asked.

The old man shook his head. 'He said nothing. Not a word. He just kept staring.'

'Creepy,' I agreed with a shudder.

The old man went on, 'I really lost my temper. I called out, "What in God's name do you want?" And that's when he stopped and sighed. Tears were running down his face and he spoke slowly ... "I couldn't speak until you asked me in the name of God. I was a boatman down the Ely River. I was buried near where I used to row my ferry. But the grave was shallow, and time has washed away the earth. When the soil washed away you could see my skull above the surface. Whoever saw that should have buried me again – except when those people are Cardiff boys in need of a rugby ball."'

I gasped. 'You don't mean to say...'

And the old moan moaned, 'Yes. The boys pulled his skull from the ground and used it to practise their kicking and passing. Have you any idea how that must have tortured the boatman's spirit?'

I agreed, 'It would do your head in...'

The old man didn't laugh. He went on, 'He said he couldn't rest till his head was buried. He'd show me where it was. I went with him, down to the river. The boys were still laughing and playing. They were big lads too. I was afraid of what they might do to me. But when I shouted they dropped their ball and ran.'

I sighed, 'That was lucky.'

But he explained, 'I think they may have seen the boatman by my side. Anyway, I picked up the skull and took it to the place he showed me. I buried it deep in the riverbank. Then, when I turned around, the figure had gone. May his poor soul rest in peace.'

There was a deep silence apart from the crackling of the logs on the fire and the moaning of the cold wind outside the darkened window.

And that is supposed to be a true story.

DID YOU KNOW...?

In 1884 Cardiff was one of the first places in Britain to come up with a new way of dealing with the dead. That happened after the Welsh Druid, Dr Williams Price, was put on trial in Cardiff, for burning the body of his dead son. He was found not guilty. After the Cardiff trial cremation was made legal in Britain.

But don't worry; it is illegal to set fire to a child if they are still alive.

CARDIFF GHOST STORY 4 – CATHEDRAL CLOSE

Cathedral Close used to be known as the 'Road of the Dead'.

Bodies were carried down this street and taken to a graveyard near the river Taff. The graveyard isn't there any more BUT people say they've seen young children in ancient clothes, laughing and playing on the road. They are said to be children who died horribly in the 1840s when the cholera epidemic broke out in Cardiff.

LAW AND DISORDER

The docks brought in riches from around the world. And where there are riches, there are thieves who want to steal them.

And where there are thieves, there are fights about the loot. The docks were a violent place in the 1800s.

PATHETIC POLICE

The police kept out of the docks.

The owners of the rich cargoes paid their own private police force to look after the goods. These special dock police were police armed with swords, not truncheons.

The thieves were well known to the police, and many had nicknames like…

- Bob the Goose
- Oily Morgan
- James Bond
(no, honest)

The police had to be as rough and tough as the villains. And, like the villains, they spent a lot of time in the pubs, drinking beer not orange juice. Sometimes they drank too much. A true story may have been reported like this…

LORD BUTE'S CARDIFF DOCK POLICE

Sergeant's Report

On the night of Tuesday 9 November, two constables, Rees and Evans, went on patrol by the docks. It was a cold night, and they visited some public houses in search of thieves. They had to take a strong drink to keep themselves warm. At five minutes past midnight, I went to the docks to inspect them.

PC Rees sounded drunk as he greeted me. 'It's a nice night isn't it, Sergeant?' he said.

'Lovely, Constable. Lovely,' I agreed.

'Dark, mind you,' Rees said wisely.

'It often is at night,' I said sarcastically.

'Yes, I've noticed that,' he replied in amazement.

'In fact, it's so dark I can't even see Constable Evans,' I pointed out.

Rees gasped, 'It's funny. I can't see him, either.' He shook his head. 'Here ... I remember a big splash when we walked over the bridge at Atlantic Wharf.'

'You don't think that was Evans, do you?' I asked.

'I can't think what else it could have been. Let's run back...' Rees cried, suddenly sober.

'I've got grappling irons here,' I said picking some up from the dock. 'There's something white out there. That'll be his face. Try and reach it, Rees.'

He threw the rope with the heavy iron hook on the end, and it landed with a splash on water. It was followed by an angry quacking sound. 'Duck,' I cried.

'Why? What's coming?' Rees asked, dropping to the ground.

I replied, 'On the water. The white thing. A duck. I didn't mean duck, I meant duck.'

It looks like we've lost Evans. Poor lad. A good constable. A credit to the Force. He'll be sadly missed. Then I heard a rumbling, growling noise. It was like an animal in the bushes growling at us.

Rees and I took out our swords. On a count of three, we jumped on the creature. It was not a wild animal but a man – a drunkard asleep and snoring in the bushes. 'Shall I arrest him?' Rees asked.

'No, Rees,' I said. 'I think we've just found Evans.'

Rees and Evans have both been sacked.

- Other officers at the docks were customs men who made sure the right taxes were paid. A police constable was fined a day's wages. What was his 'crime'? He got into a snowball fight with a customs officer.

- The body of a drowned man was found rotting in Cardiff Harbour. The Bute Police dragged it out and took it to the body store – the morgue. His family went to view his body. They arrived to find the corpse had vanished. It seems the officer in charge had taken the dead body to the wrong morgue. The constable was fined a day's pay. That did not pay for the terrible upset to the family.

TERRIBLE 20TH CENTURY

The terrible twentieth century came along with two woeful World Wars. There were some places you wouldn't want to hang around. Especially Cardiff Prison. And even a museum could have a terror toilet.

NATIONAL MUSEUM CARDIFF

The town of Cardiff was made a city in 1905. In that same year the National Museum was founded. It is one of the largest museums in the United Kingdom.

FANTASTIC FACT OF CARDIFF

The man who planned the National Museum building – the architect Dunbar Smith – had his ashes buried in the building. But years later the ashes were moved to make way for a new men's toilet. Spooky Smith started moving chairs in the night. Now the awful architect haunts the loos.

CARDIFF PRISON

Cardiff has a fine prison. But not if you are inside it and not if you are hanged there.

The Cardiff Courier

WIN! Free tickets to Cardiff City's brand new museum*
*which is free anyway

WOMAN EXECUTED TODAY

Today the first, last and only woman to be hanged in Cardiff Prison has been executed.

Her crime? She was a 'baby farmer'. Her name was Rhoda Willis.

A cobbler called David Evans from Pontypool tried to run his business and look after his children when his wife left him. Rhoda Willis, a handsome woman from Sunderland in the north of England, came to care for them. She then told David Evans they could make extra money by looking after other babies as well as his own.

In March, Rhoda put an advert in a local paper:

MARRIED COUPLE WISH TO ADOPT A BABY AS THEIR OWN.
It will be given every comfort and care.
It must be healthy. A small fee must be paid.
Reply to *The Cardiff Courier* REF. CC44

A woman answered the advert. Rhoda Willis took the unwanted child from its mother and was paid £5. The child died because Rhoda didn't look after it. She took another but David Evans refused to have it in his house. Rhoda Willis smothered it.

The police were called, and the baby farmer was taken to court. A jury heard the case against her. It took them just 12 minutes to decide she was guilty and should hang.

On 14 August 1907, Rhoda Willis went calmly to her execution.

THE WOEFUL FIRST WORLD WAR

Around 1910, one of the Bute family, Lord Ninian Edward Crichton-Stuart, had a football ground named after him: Ninian Park. Ninian was a Member of Parliament – an MP.

The First World War started in 1914 and Lord Ninian Edward Crichton-Stuart went off to fight.

At the Battle of Loos in October 1915 the German enemy attacked the British trenches.

Ninian's men, the 6th Battalion, Welsh Regiment, had not slept for two days and had marched for 16 hours to reach the enemy. They captured some enemy trenches. The Germans came back to drive out the Welsh men.

The Welsh forces were divided into two and cut off. Ninian ordered his men…

Ninian had a pistol. He raised his head above the safety of the trench to fire at the enemy. A German rifleman shot him in the head.

Twenty-two British MPs died in the First World War. Ninian was the only Welsh MP to die. He was rewarded with a statue in Cardiff's Cathays Park.

THE OTHER 60,000 MEN IN THE BRITISH ARMY WHO WERE KILLED, WOUNDED OR MISSING AT THE BATTLE OF LOOS DID NOT GET STATUES

THE 842 MEN IN NINIAN'S BATTALION STARTED FIGHTING IN THE WAR IN 1914. WHEN IT ENDED IN 1918, ONLY 30 WERE LEFT. THEY DIDN'T GET STATUES EITHER

It just goes to show that you can't shoot a Bute without remembering him in a statue.

Ninian Park football ground was knocked down in 2009.

DID YOU KNOW...?

The German airships – Zeppelins – dropped bombs on British towns in the First World War.

But in 1915, Cardiff children were ready for an attack if it had come. A poster told them...

WHEN ZEPPELIN ATTACKS COME

- The alarm for a Zeppelin attack will be a gong, a police whistle and a loud electric bell, all to be used together.

- This will be followed by a pause and one blast of a horn – known as the 'Special Signal'.

- Pupils on the top floor of the school must run in single file downstairs and march smartly in corridors

- They must remain in the shelters until the all-clear is sounded

Cardiff schools practised these. No bombs were dropped, and no one was killed running down the stairs. No one went deaf from 'a gong, a police whistle and a loud electric bell' all being used together.

But Cardiff people were afraid. And some people reported raids that never happened.

HUNGRY YEARS

In the 1930s there were very few jobs, and the workers of Cardiff became terribly poor. Many began to starve.

There was a hunger march to London to protest against the conditions – it didn't do much good.

SECOND WORLD WAR

The First World War saw a lot of Cardiff men die on the green fields of France. But when the Second World War started you didn't have to travel across the English Channel to be killed. You could just sit at home and the enemy would drop bombs on you.

Some of the stories to come out of the war are horrible…

THE CARDIFF TIMES

3 January 1941

FREE NAZI BOMBER IDENTIFICATION CHART INSIDE

DEADLY RAID ON STOCKLAND STREET

Last night was a full moon, or a Bombers' Moon as they are now known. That moonlight showed the way for around 100 German planes to raid Cardiff. The raid went on for more than ten hours.

One of the worst incidents was at the Hollyman Brothers Bakery on the corner of Corporation Road and Stockland Street. The bakery cellar had been used as an air-raid shelter but took a direct hit. The bomb went through the roof and the floors above and ended up on the floor of the cellar.

The 32 people in the shelter, including the Hollyman family, were killed.

Bakery in ruins

The shop was rebuilt after the war and went on as a bakery for about ten years before it closed.

It is now a shop called Clarence Hardware and on the side of the building you can see a plaque to remember the 32 victims of that raid.

Other bombs fell that night and damaged Llandaff Cathedral. In the graveyard bones were blown into the sky.

The west of Cardiff was the worst-hit area. One hundred and sixteen men, women and children were killed, with 50 of them dying in one street, De Burgh Street.

There were different sorts of shelters to go to, like Anderson shelters in people's gardens. But they couldn't save people when a powerful bomb landed too close.

Ten people from the Palmer family in Cathays died in their Anderson shelter when a bomb struck. Near by, the church hall at Wyverne Road was flattened, but the Boy Scouts' flag was saved from the rubble. Why was the scout flag so precious?
a) It had been carried by Captain Scott when he explored the South Pole 30 years before

b) It had been saved from the *Titanic* when it sank 30 years before

c) It had been used to wrap the body of Llywelyn Bren after his execution

Answer: **a)** Of course, Captain Scott reached the Antarctic but he and his explorers died in the icy storms as they tried to get back. He was a British hero. The Cardiff scout leader in 1910 gave the flag to Captain Scott when his Antarctic ship stopped off in Cardiff for coal. The explorer took it with him. The flag probably stayed at Scott's base camp in the Antarctic. It never reached the South Pole and was returned to the Cardiff Scouts. You can see it in Cardiff Museum.

EVANS ABOVE

Captain Scott needed money to pay for his trip to the South Pole – all the sledges and ponies, the food and the tents, as well as hiring the *Terra Nova* ship to get the explorers there.

One of Scott's Antarctic team was Teddy Evans. Teddy's grandfather may have been born in Cardiff. So, Scott sent Teddy Evans to Cardiff to raise some of the £50–60,000 that the expedition needed.

By December 1909 Teddy had raised £1,500 by going around doing talks.

READY, TEDDY, GO...
TO ANTARCTICA

TUESDAY EVENING AT 7 P.M.
Come to Cardiff City Hall to hear about the world's greatest adventure

Cardiff's own Teddy Evans will talk about Captain Scott's trip to the Antarctic

Entry: one shilling to hear about the trip to the ice paradise

Free penguin to the buyer of the first ticket*

*If Captain Scott gets back alive he will bring a penguin back with him

In June 1910 Captain Scott himself arrived in Cardiff on board the *Terra Nova* ship that would be heading for the Antarctic.

Captain Scott and his officers were given a wonderful farewell feast at the Royal Hotel in St. Mary's Street. (The ordinary crewmen had to eat at the Barry Hotel which was far less grand.)

By now Cardiff people had raised £2,500 – far more than any other town in Britain. *Terra Nova* set sail with the flags of Cardiff and Wales flying from the masts. Fastened to the front of the ship was the little green Cardiff Boy Scouts' flag.

TRICKY TARGETS

In the Second World War enemy bombers wanted to hit Cardiff Docks and wreck the British ships of course. The Royal Air Force sent up fighter planes to try to shoot down the bombers. So, the enemy bombers came back to hit the airfields where the Cardiff fighter planes were based.

These decoys were empty fields so the bombs would do no harm except to Welsh worms and sad sheep. But the decoys had to be secret. If the enemy knew where the make-believe sites were, they would not waste their bombs on them.

So, how do you make a decoy airfield?

Cardiff had three decoy sites. One of the sites worked and drew enemy bombers away from Cardiff Docks. Three bombs were dropped and saved damage to the ships. Sadly, they wrecked a farmhouse where two sisters were living.

Many of these decoy fields were still there years after the war had finished. The farmers took them back and had to destroy the dummies.

EPILOGUE

Just about everyone in history must have thought that life would go on the same way for ever more.

Just about everyone was wrong.

The people of Cardiff probably thought their city would send Welsh coal around the world for ever more.

Before the First World War began in 1914, Cardiff Docks were the busiest port in the world. Ten million tonnes of coal went through those docks.

In 1964 – just fifty years later – that amount of coal was down. But down to what?

a)   Eight million tonnes
b)   Four million tonnes
c)   Zero million tonnes

Answer: c) In 1964 West Bute Dock closed as the last shipment of coal left the docks.

The city's steel-making went the same way. In 1938 Cardiff's steelworks were making three million tonnes of steel. Forty years later it closed.

The world has moved on. Cardiff has moved with it. Mostly for the better. In 1955 Cardiff was made capital city of the whole of Wales. It was the start of a new age. Coal and steel had turned the little village of Cardiff into a great city. The choking smoke of industry has gone but Cardiff keeps growing without it.

The history of the world has been horrible with its burnings and hangings, famines and plagues. There is one person out there who can make the future much better. Not just for Cardiff but the whole world.

INTERESTING INDEX

Where will you find cholera, Death Junction and the Battle of Loos in an index? In a Horrible Histories book, of course!

- Act of Union 52, 54
- Alice, Princess 73-4
- Angles and Saxons 22-3, 24, 25, 27
- Anne, Queen 75
- Antarctic expedition 112, 113-15
- Arnold, John (judge) 64, 66
- Australia, transportation to 82, 83

- 'baby farming' 105-6
- beheadings 11, 17-18, 50, 51
- Bevan, Aneurin (politician) 78-9
- bombing raids 108, 111-12, 115-16, 117
- Borrow, George (writer) 84
- Boy Scouts' flag 112-13, 115
- Boyle, John 92-3
- brains, preservation of 18
- Brigantes tribe 15
- Bristol Channel 41, 63
- bull-baiting 79-80
- burgage plots 61
- burial customs 97
- burial in sand 72
- burning at the stake 55, 56, 57, 58, 72
- Bute, 2nd Marquess of 77, 93
- Bute, 3rd Marquess of 19, 20, 38, 92, 93
- Buttington, Battle of 27

- Caer-Taff (old name for Cardiff) 16
- Caerau Hillfort 10, 11, 13, 19, 74
- Caerphilly Castle 73, 74
- Callis, John (pirate) 54, 60-1
- canals 77
- capital city status 7, 120-1
- Capital Tower 53
- Capper, Thomas (Protestant martyr) 55-6
- Caratacus (Celtic Briton) 12, 13, 14, 15, 17

Cardiff Bay 25, 90
Cardiff Castle 19-20, 30, 32, 33-5, 38, 57, 92-3
Cardiff Docks 19, 76, 77, 78, 98-9, 102, 115, 117, 120
Cardiff Prison 66, 103, 105
Cardiff Royal Infirmary 91
Cartimandua, Queen 15
Castell Coch ('Red Castle') 35, 37-9
Cathays Park 108
Cathedral Close 97
Catholics 52, 55, 56, 57, 63-8, 74, 86
Catuvellauni tribe 12
Celtic Britons 10-18, 19
Charles I, King 38, 72
cholera 86-90, 91, 97
city status 104
Claudius (Roman emperor) 17
coal mining and miners 45-6, 76-8, 80, 83, 84, 90, 120
cremation 97
Crichton-Stuart, Lord Ninian Edward 106-8
Crockherbtown Lane 23
customs officers 102

Dark Ages 22, 25
David, St 23-4
Death Junction 63-4, 68
decoy airfields 116-18
Dolphyn, Colyn (pirate) 71-2
drunkenness 78, 99, 100, 101

eagles (treasure guards) 39
Edward I, King 44
Edward VI, King 56
Elizabeth I, Queen 59, 60, 62
English Civil War 38, 72, 74
English language 54
Evans, Philip (Catholic priest and martyr) 63-8
Evans, Teddy (polar explorer) 113-14

Evesham, Battle of 36

famine 43, 86
ferryman, ghost of the 94-6
First World War 107-9, 110
Fitzhamon, Robert (Norman) 30
football 106, 108

gangs 78
George I, King 75
Georgians 75-84
ghost stories 20, 32, 37, 38, 61, 74, 87-96, 97, 104
Gloucester, Earls of 30, 34, 35-7
Gloucester, Lady 33, 34-5
Great Flood 63
Greyfriars Monastery 23, 46, 53
guerrilla warfare 14

hangings 68, 81, 83, 105, 106
hanging, drawing and quartering 44, 64, 67-8
Hastings, Marquess of 92-3
Henry I, King 30, 31, 32
Henry III, King 36
Henry VII, King (Henry Tudor) 48-9, 50
Henry VIII, King 52-3, 55, 56
Hollyman Brothers Bakery 111
hunger march 110

Ifor Bach (Ivor the Short - rebel) 33-5, 38, 41
Ireland 21, 86
ironworkers 78, 80, 81-2, 90

Jasper Tower 52
Jasper Tudor (uncle of Henry VII) 49-52, 53
Jews, attack on 36
John, King 35
Jones, Rice 58

Keynsham Abbey 52
kidnappings 33-5, 72

leaning tower, Caerphilly Castle 74
leek (symbol of Wales) 24
Llandaff Cathedral 52, 112
Llandough Hospital 92
Lloyd, John (Catholic priest and martyr) 63-8
Llywelyn Bren (rebel) 41-5, 46, 53
Loos, Battle of 107-8
Lord of Cardiff 49-50, 52

MacRae, Lady Margaret 93
Magna Carta 35
Mary, Queen 56, 57, 58
Matilda (wife of William the Conqueror) 31-2
Matt of the Iron Hand (wrecker) 69, 70-1
Merthyr 80-1, 83
Middle Ages 40-7
Millennium Stadium 56
monasteries 23, 46, 52, 53
monks 12, 23, 24, 25-7, 52
Montfort, Simon de (noble rebel) 36

National Health Service 78
National Museum Cardiff 104, 113
Ninian Park 106, 108
Normans 28, 29-37

Owain Glyndwr (Welsh hero) 46, 47
Owen, George (historian) 59

Parker, Ieuan 83
Payne de Turberville (Norman) 45
Penderyn, Dic (rioter) 80, 81, 82-3
Peterston-super-Ely 47
pirates 41, 54, 59-61, 71-2
police 78, 98-102
Price, Dr Williams (Welsh Druid) 97

Protestants 52, 55, 56, 58

railways 77
Red Dragon 7, 8
'Red Earl' (7th Earl of Gloucester) 35-7, 39
Rhymney, River 25
Richard III, King 49
riots and rebellions 21, 41-4, 45-7, 72, 78, 80-3
Road of the Dead 97
Robert II of Normandy 30-1, 32
Romans 11-17, 19, 22
Roundheads 72, 74
Rummer Tavern 61

sagas 25, 26-7
St. David's Cathedral 23
St. Fagan, Battle of 72
St. Mary Street 57, 63, 81, 83, 114
Scapula, Publius Ostorius (Roman general) 13-14, 15-16
Scott, Captain (polar explorer) 112, 113, 114
Second World War 39, 110-12, 115-18
secret passage (Castle Coch to Cardiff Castle) 38
Silures tribe 13, 14, 16, 19
slavery 25
Smith, Dunbar (architect) 104
steam trains 77
steelworks 120
street brawls 54, 78
Stuarts 62-74, 75

Tacitus (Roman historian) 15
Taff, River 25, 32, 56, 63, 97
tennis 58, 66
Terra Nova (ship) 113, 114, 115
Tew Teg 73
thieves 69, 98-9

Thomas, Megan 87-9, 90-1
Thomas, Tegwyn 87-9, 90-1
Thornbury 53
treasure, hidden 38-9
trials 41-4, 65-6, 97, 106
tsunami wave 63
Tudors 48-61

Vaughan, Walter (wrecker) 69, 70-1
Victoria, Queen 76, 84, 85

Victorians 85-102
Vikings 23, 25-8

White, Rawlins (Protestant martyr) 56-8
William the Conqueror 29-32
William IV, King 85
Willis, Rhoda ('baby farmer') 105-6
wreckers 69, 70-1

Zeppelins 108-9

TERRY DEARY

Terry Deary was born at a very early age, so long ago he can't remember. But his mother, who was there at the time, says he was born in Sunderland, northeast England, in 1946 – so it's not true that he writes all *Horrible Histories* from memory. At school he was a horrible child only interested in playing football and giving teachers a hard time. His history lessons were so boring and so badly taught, that he learned to loathe the subject. *Horrible Histories* is his revenge.

MARTIN BROWN

Martin Brown was born in Melbourne, on the proper side of the world. Ever since he can remember he's been drawing. His dad used to bring back huge sheets of paper from work and Martin would fill them with doodles and little figures. Then, quite suddenly, with food and water, he grew up, moved to the UK and found work doing what he's always wanted to do: drawing doodles and little figures.

WHY NOT READ!

INTRODUCTION

Imagine living in a country where the trees drip with human blood.

A country where dragons are out to roast you for dinner.

And where lords invite you to dinner so they can massacre you.

A country invaded by Viking sea-raiders from the west. They smash down your churches or set fire to them if you try to hide inside.

Country cottage to rent

May include unexpected guests*

***Vikings**

★ RHODRI'S ★ DRAGON RACE

New series, out now

WHICH DRAGON WILL BE THE FASTEST, WHILE BEING THE MOST GLAMOROUS?

And then Norman knights from the east arrive and build castles and churches (and kill a few peasants who get in their way).

It's a country where gangs of murdering robbers attack you as you walk through their forests.

A country where the punishment for stealing cattle is to have your arms cut off and the punishment for a servant who steals from her mistress is to be burned alive.

Where is this hideously horrible place? Transylvania in the reign of Dracula?

No.

Germany in the fairy tales of the Brothers Grimm?

No.

The prize for guessing is £1000[1].

Here are some clues to help you...

---

1. If you guessed correctly please send the £1000 to me, Terry Deary, care of the publisher. Thank you.

Yes, the horrible country is...

...Wales[2]!

The GOOD news is the trees no longer drip with blood and the dragons have disappeared ... probably killed off by knights in fireproof knickers. The Vikings have stopped raiding and you can steal as many cattle as you like without having your arms cut off.

All those things happened in Wales's horrible history.

So if you want to know all about these dreadful deeds (not to mention killer squirrels) then read on!

---

2. You probably cheated and read it on the cover of this book. In that case the prize is doubled to £2000. Please send it as soon as possible because I am a penniless author.

EARLY TIMELINE

The Welsh are the descendants of the ancient Britons. These Celtic tribes ruled most of Britain till the Romans barged in.

Wales hasn't always been horrible. It was quite pleasant in 1306 and again in 1972. But here are some of the horrible highlights…

230,000 BC Neanderthal creatures wander the hills of Wales. They look like humans but act like apes. (Now we call them football supporters.)

- AD 43 Roman Emperor Claudius orders an invasion of Britain. The Romans drive the Britons out of England. The only place the Brits can go is west – to Wales. Among them is Caratacus who was from the Catuvellauni tribe, north-west of London. He is defeated in England.

- 48 Caratacus stirs up the Silures tribe down in South Wales. He becomes one of the first-ever Welsh heroes. He attacks Roman supplies, and robs and murders tribes (like the Dubonni) who dare to make friends with the Romans.

- 75 The Romans rule Wales.

313 Christianity has started to take over as top religion in Wales. The ancient Welsh priests, the 'Druids', are on the way out ... along with their human sacrifices.

410 The Romans leave. Saxon invaders attack. The Welsh in the south are battered. The ones in the mountains are bothered.

496 Brit hero King Arthur battles the Saxons at Mount Badon. Did Arthur really rule or is he just a story? And was he Welsh? Who knows. This is also the time of saints. Welsh saints set up sites in Wales to teach Christianity.

— **589** Bishop David dies. He will live on as Saint David ... the patron saint of Wales.

RIP DAVE

— **606** The Welsh Christians argue with the Pope. St Augustine is sent from Rome to sort them out. St Gus says:

If the Welsh will not have peace with us, they shall die at the hands of the Saxons.

WE'RE VERY RELIGIOUS

Sure enough, Saxon king Ethelfrith massacres thousands of Welsh at Chester. He kills 1,200 Welsh monks too – just for fun.

— **784** Offa of Mercia is a powerful Saxon king. He builds Offa's Dyke, marking Wales's eastern border. The Dyke is just a long mound of earth. But Welsh who cross it risk their lives.

CROSS THIS AND IT'S OFF-A WITH YOUR HEAD

GET OFF-A THE MOUND!

- **850** First report of a Viking attack on Wales. They kill King Cyngen. The Welsh need a hero to unite them. And they find one in the great Rhodri Mawr.

- **878** Rhodri Mawr dies fighting the English. He was the first Welsh ruler to unite the Welsh tribes under one rule. During his reign, the Vikings increase their raids.

- **927** Welsh kings give in and allow the English to be their king of kings.

- **1039** The last of the Welsh High Kings, Gruffydd ap Llywelyn, takes the throne. By 1057 he has battled and murdered his way to all the thrones of Wales.

- **1063** Gruffydd beaten by Harold of England then murdered … probably by his own men.

HEADS AND TAILS

The ancient Welsh had a thing about heads. A lot of their legends were about heads ... usually dead heads.

HEAD BOY BRAN

In the Welsh legends the greatest Welshman was Bendigeidfran ... or Bran for short. Well, when I say 'short' he was really 'long'. He was so tall he paddled across the Irish Sea to fight the Irish.

Why would he want to attack the Irish?
Because they insulted his sister, Branwen.
Here is her terrible tale…

> Once upon a time there was a lovely Welsh princess called Branwen. She was so lovely the Irish King Matholwch wanted to marry her. Beautiful Branwen said, 'Yes … please.' (You should always say 'please'.)
>
> But Branwen's nasty brother was so jealous he attacked the Irish king's horses … nastily. He sliced their lips back to their teeth, and their ears back to their heads, and their tails to their backs – and wherever he could get a grip on their eyelids, he would cut these back to the bone. That was nasty, wasn't it?
>
> Matholwch felt a real fool so he took Branwen back to Ireland and punished her. He made her slave in the kitchens and sent a butcher to slap her around the head every day. Poor princess. So the brave Branwen tamed a starling to sit on the edge of her bread bowl. Let's hope it didn't poop in the pastry! She taught it to talk.
>
> 'Starling,' she said, 'fly to Wales and tell my big brothers how unhappy I am.'
>
> 'Squawk,' said the starling.
>
> Brother Bendigeidfran walked over from Wales while the rest of the army went in ships. The Welsh massacred every living Irish person except for five Irish women. The Irish killed every Welsh soldier except seven heroes. Even Bran died with a poisoned spear in his foot. As he died he told

his brothers, 'Cut off my head and take it home to Britain. Bury it in London and I will protect the country from danger.'

Then the heroes took Branwen home along with Brother Bran's big head.

What a happy ending!

No.

Branwen landed at the Welsh island of Anglesey and looked back at Ireland. She wept, 'Oh, Ireland. Everyone massacred ... Except five women who are expecting babies.' Then she looked at Wales and wept. 'Oh, ohhhh! Britain! All the greatest warriors dead ... Except the seven warriors who brought Bran's head home. Woe to me that I was ever born. Two good islands have been ruined because of me.' Then she looked at her brothers and wept, 'Oh, I think I will die of a broken heart.'

And that's just what she did! They buried her.

Sorry but we don't know what happened to the starling.

The End

Starling for sale
FULLY TRAINED
Cash only

Bran's head was buried in London. But someone stole it along with two other skulls from the graveyard and so Britain was never safe again.

The law officers never found out who stole those three skulls.

This may sound like a silly story. But it tells us something about the Celts who lived in Wales in ancient times…

COLLECT THEM ALL!

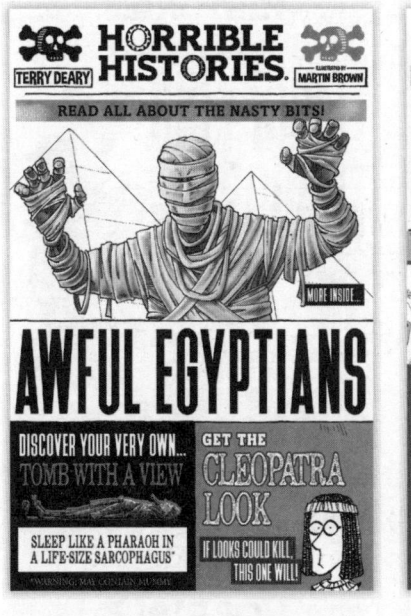

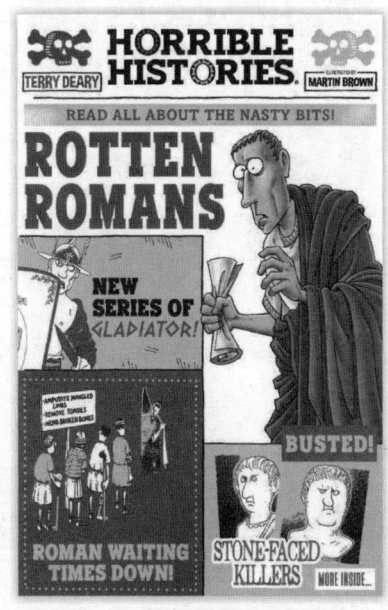

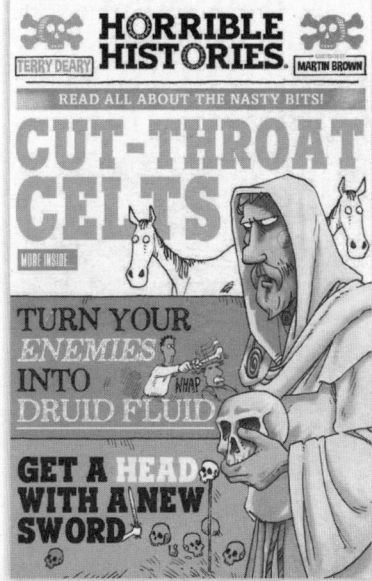

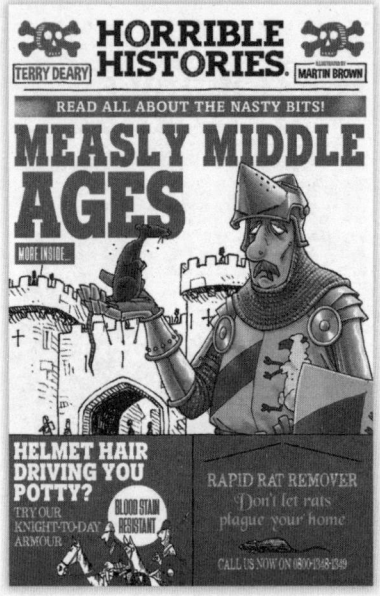